7 Steps to Re-Invent Yourself

"The Art of Getting Un-Stuck"

Bradley Kelley

Seven Steps to Re-Invent Yourself is available on Amazon and Kindle

You may also purchase Seven Steps to Re-Invent Yourself at www.lifetransformationscoaching.com

Special prices for bulk quantities, please contact Life Transformation Coaching at 405-343-1535

ISBN 9781979633574

Bradley Kelley is a Founding Member of The Les Brown Maximum Achievement Team and Founder of Life Transformation Coaching (Changing the World One Dream at A Time)

Just when you think your stuck, you find hope given from the Grace of the Father.

Foreward by Lawrence Neisent

A few years ago I had the privilege of meeting Bradley Kelley. As we began to speak I could sense a great purpose coming from deep pain in his life. His transparency and vibrancy caught my attention causing me to see the gift of leadership and influence God has given him to carry. I've observed as people around him reference him as a mentor and even a father.

Brad's writing brings an expression of authenticity and inspiration as he shares his journey of walking through difficulty and refusing to give in. There were many reasons in his life to pick up his feet and just be swept downstream to a disappointed conclusion in life. Instead we see a man who has chosen to dig in and fight the current making his way against the stream and choosing to take others with him to higher ground. Everybody has a story and Brad has chosen to share his story to encourage the rest of us to discover dignity and significance in the life we live.

Thank you for your courage to share your story with us Brad.

Introduction

If you think about where you've been, where you are, and where you're going, does it line up with the dreams you had as a child? For many of us, myself included, I am no-where near where I thought I would be at 46. You see, the truth is, life has a way of pulling us different directions other than that of our goals and dreams we develop in our youth. Simply put, "Life Happens"! In today's world, the hardships, struggles, and pain seem to direct our future, and without a well-defined plan of action, we are lead down a different path, and seem to never re-direct our life's plan, therefore leaving us stuck. It's a place I have so often ended up, and am quite familiar with, being "Stuck". I have always been able to re-direct my path, but I did it alone, and never ended up where I wanted to be.

Colossians 1:16 Everything got started in Him and finds its purpose in Him.

Don't do it alone. Seek out mentors, be it a Spiritual Mentor, a Financial Mentor, or Father Figure Mentor. **Proverbs 15:22 Plans go wrong for lack of advice; many advisers bring success.** This scripture resonates deep in my soul where I know only the true beauty lies, and it allows me each day to turn to the one's I trust the most when trying to make any decision that will direct my future. Massive action with a successful result requires methodical preludes of decisions, never should it be done alone.

A renewing of the mind is something that a lot of us will require to pull the very best out of ourselves, and work towards our full potential that we desire and long for. It is all too often that we become conformed to the world and just go along with ways of our up-bringing and never getting out the cycles of our past. All the while knowing that what we are doing isn't really, in fact, what we want to be doing or should be doing. It's time that we get out of our old nature and step into the new and refocus our direction and rediscover our purpose. God's purpose!

It is time to get serious about where you were, where you are, and where you want to be and make the change that you have been avoiding for so many years. By no means is it going to be easy, because change never is, but it is going to be well worth it. Tell yourself every day that "change is scary at first, messy in the middle, but glorious at the end"! The first time I heard those words was from the Queen of Motivation, Miss. Ona Brown, that's right, Les Brown's baby girl. It is something that has stuck with me and I refer to it quite often, change isn't easy, but it is possible.

Bradley Kelley

Table of Contents

Chapter 1 "Let Go, Let God, Find your Peace"

There comes a point in our lives when we must submit to self-reflection and face many destructive giants of our past. All too many times through life, we seem to live in the past, and let it direct our path to our future. We live on a life built with "what if's", and "should have's", instead of, "that was then, and this is now". Speaking from an expert in making mistakes, I have felt this feeling of helplessness throughout my entire life. I am not saying that, "my entire life was directed by mistakes", because there are many victories and beautiful things that have come from my past, but, if

I would have "taken action" at every turning point in my life, the outcome would have been much more glorious.

Not letting go seems to be one of the biggest issues that prevent many from truly experiencing success in many areas of life. If we hold on to the past, how can we achieve our greatness from within? Our past doesn't define who we are, it's just a mere reflection of where we've been. If you think about it, we are all the same, but each one of us has been given a different path to walk. Each path's footsteps planted before they are even taken. Me personally, I am on a journey, both spiritual and physical. And for years I lived a life of what if's, and why didn't I do this instead of that. Do you want to guess where that got me? That's right, stuck in the same old place that lead me to a brick wall with no dreams or goals, and no desire to better myself.

If we can honestly look at life as a process of progress, and not as perfection, just imagine how far along we would be when it comes to achieving our dreams and goals. "Letting Go" is the 1st part of re-inventing yourself. It's time to forgive those that need to be forgiven, and ask for forgiveness from those that need to forgive us. Most of all, we must forgive ourselves.

For 19 years of my adult life I lived with a grudge against my father, and that was after he had passed away. I was mad at him for the way that he was and all that I saw growing up as a kid. Don't get me wrong, there were some positive lessons that came from my youth, but there were also many instances that led me to being angry at him for what he had done. Little did I know or realize that it wasn't his fault.

You see, when my father returned from Vietnam, only a shell of a man returned. He was beaten, tattered, and broken from what he encountered there. This was before "PTSD" was diagnosed and given a name, and I have been around people returning from war and have also seen in them some of the same issues and traits as my father's, and they were also diagnosed with "PTSD", except his never seemed to stop. It was a continuous suffering with no breaks in the middle, which made him literally soulless. He was still able to show some affection, but usually to others rather than those of us in his immediate family.

My father was never able to let go of his past, which in return led him down a path of anger and destruction. Not one time in his life did I ever hear or see him pray, or step foot in a church, unless it was a wedding or a funeral, but even then, he seemed to be very anxious about being in that type of surrounding, unless he was drinking. Which was quite often. I often think back, again, with a "what if attitude", he had received treatment, and had medical help with his issues, and was able to let go of his past. What kind of man would I have had to look up to as a father? One with whom I could seek guidance from, advice from when I hit many of my roadblocks in life, and just someone who would listen to me with a sober ear and a fresh spirit.

The day my father passed away was a day that I will never forget. December 24th, 1997. It was a day of sadness, bitterness, and anger. You see, I was finally able to release all the pain of the past from my mind, and focus on being a better man than what I saw in him, but it also made me bitter and angry because of the last conversation that I had with him. You see on October 31st, of the same year, my father and mother watched my children while we were planning to go to a Halloween party. Then suddenly the phone rang, it was my mother, telling me I needed to come pick up my children and as that last word of the sentence came from her mouth, I heard a slap! It sounded as if someone took the palm of their hand, slapping it on wet skin. It was a sound I will never forget, and then I heard the phone hit the floor. I instantly fled out the door and rushed over to their house, and without saying a word, I tried to pull my father out of the front door by his hair ready for a fight. I am thankful that my mother and wife at the time, could stop me, because I am certain that I would have done something that I would have regretted the rest of my life. That was the very last time that I spoke to my father and he past-away two months later. That was the start of my 19-year-old grudge!

Truth is, the moment before he took his last breath, and after being unconscious for 3 solid days, he opened his eyes and said to me. "I'm sorry"! Too hurt to realize it, and to mad to care, that was his way of trying to find his peace before he journeyed over into the other side, and make amends for all he had done. He had finally been able to let go, but unfortunately it was on his death bed. My father was 48 years old when he passed, and he lived life showered with pain and disgrace from what he did and encountered in Vietnam. If only I would have realized it back then, that his issues weren't who he wanted to be, but were in fact developed through his life events, then maybe I would have been mature enough to handle each situation differently. With a loving heart, and not expecting anything in return.

Now, think about your life and what you've been through! Who has put you through it? Who have you put through it? What events took place that got you stuck? What is it that is sticking to you like glue? What are you holding onto that you just can't forget about? What past events are holding you back from your greatness? Who do you blame your struggles on? Who do you blame your failures on? Trust me, I've done all of this, way too often, and still ended up with the same result. A result of mediocrity and failure! Now, look in the mirror, what do you see? That person staring back at you may very well be the problem!

It's time to re-invent yourself! It's time to let go! It's finally time for you to start enjoying all the little things in life that you have been missing for so many years. You are the only one that can forgive all the pain of the past, and God is the only one whom can take you to where you want to be. It's time to let go, and let God! **Proverbs 15:13 A glad heart makes a happy face; a broken heart crushes the spirit.** Don't you think it's time for some healing? A healing of the heart. It's time to let God be the pilot, and for you to just relax and enjoy the ride. For years I never really thought about or realized what that phrase meant. "Let go, and Let God". I wanted to be in control, and I blamed everything in my life on those around me, and as well, as on God. I never took responsibility for my own actions nor did I consider the fact that it was me who was making all the decisions. All the bad decisions. Because I never really knew God. I never really thought about those around me and how my decisions would affect their lives as well as mine. You could say that I lived a selfish life and never really cared about anyone other than myself!

In order, to truly "Let God" take control of your life, you need to embark on a spiritual journey and be open to the change that He wants to make in your life. It will also require the ability to accept the fact that you are no longer in it for your own selfish needs, but for the needs of others around you. Having a "Servants Heart", is where true leadership and love come from and as well as the definition of "Finding Peace". Isn't it time that you seek out true peace? Let go of all the hurt of the past and then you will finally be able to, "Let Go, and Let God"? Everything you are reading sounds like a really good plan, doesn't it? But a plan without action is merely a thought. I hear people say, every day, "I wish things were different"! "Why can't I get it right"! And "If I had done this I would have been more successful"! Stop with all the negative self-talk, it's time to act! It's time to step up and turn it over, and I mean turn everything over. It's time to "Let Go, and Let God" and finally find some "Peace".

Jim Rohn said it best, "If you want things to change, you must change"! Think about that quote for a moment, does it make sense to you? Do you feel a sense of urgency to make the change that you want to see? Be the change that you want to see in this world, and I guarantee every part of your life will improve. Your relationships with your family, your friends, your job, your co-workers, and most importantly, Christ. Or, you can just sit there, doing the same thing that you have always done, expecting different results, but nothing ever changing, or getting better. Think about the true definition of insanity. "Doing the same thing over and over and expecting different results". The bible says, **"anyone who holds on to life just as it is destroys that life. But if you let it go, you'll have it forever, real and eternal". Excerpt from "The Purpose**

Driven Life". It's time to step outside of your comfort zone, and start the process of change. So, what are you waiting for? Now that we have your wheels spinning inside your head, it's time to develop a game plan, and develop a hunger for your life to change. You are about to do a complete 180-degree turn and start focusing on your future and quit living in the past. Are you ready? Do you have that burning desire? Are those around you counting on you to bring out your greatness so they can look up to you the way God intended, are you ready to see your greatness revealed? Then let's continue! Open your mind for this journey, and together, start the re-invention process.

Exercise:

1.With whom do you need to forgive?

_____

_____

_____

_____

_____

2. With whom do you need forgiveness

from?

_____

_____

_____

_____

_____

3. What are you holding onto that you just

can't forget about?

_____

_____

_____

_____

_____

4. What past events are holding you back

from your greatness?

_____

_____

_____

_____

_____

5. List one major event that got you stuck?

_____

_____

_____

_____

_____

6. Who do you blame your failures on?

_____

_____

_____

_____

_____

For us to grow in life, we must accept responsibility for our own actions and what we have put ourselves through. Until you can honestly say that I am not in control of my own destiny, but am in that of my actions, you will never experience your true calling for greatness. If you answered question six with any one's name other than your own, then you are missing the point. The best thing I ever told my children was not to regret any decision that you ever make, we are free to make our own decisions in life and if you do, you will live a life of regrets. If we learn from our mistakes, and in fact use it as a growth

opportunity then we will get so much

further in life. You can finally "Let Go, Let

God, and Find Peace"!

Chapter 2 "Learning the Art of Discipline"

Step 2 is going to re-direct your thinking and bring to life some of the things you know you should be doing, but are not. By no means will this be an easy process for you to just make a switch, but, the end result will lead you to being more confident in your everyday life and enable you to strive to bring out the best in what you do and how you live.

Do you live a disciplined life? Do you have what it takes to make the right decisions that will leave a lasting, positive footprint everywhere you go? Your finances, health, personal relationships, business relationships, spiritual connections, and your legacy? Being disciplined means that you need to possess self-control. Reverting from all the things that you know you shouldn't do, but still lack the self-control to do what is right. Society seems to set the standard today for self-discipline, creating bad habits through TV, social media, and simply being out and part of the public. It is something that so many of us fall short of these days in our day to day lives, but it is never too late to redirect our thinking and retrain our minds to do what is right. We all live with a certain standard of ethics and beliefs that have been instilled in our lives through the years. But somewhere down the line, we lost the aspect of self-control and discipline in our lives.

"If we don't discipline ourselves, then the world will do it for us".

William Feather

These are questions I often ask myself these days. For many years I never really thought about being disciplined. I knew that I wanted things to change, but that was just it, I wanted them to change without putting the work in. I didn't realize that for things to change, I had to change! I know that I lived with discipline, but I lived life on my terms and no one else's. I ate what I wanted, when I wanted and never worried about the lasting effects of fast food or the portions that I put into my body would have on my health. I had no routine when it came to exercise and was in the worst shape of my life at almost 300 lbs. I had no cares about how I felt or the lasting impact it had on my health.

I partied and drank too much, leaving negative footprints on my family and friends everywhere I went. The damage I inflicted on my body with drugs and alcohol started at a very young age for me and it lasted for over 2 decades. By the Grace of God, I am still healthy with no known health issues as of today. One could say that I was being protected by my higher power, Jesus Christ, for many years. Which tells me that my purpose has been reignited and we will go more into "purpose" later on in the following chapters.

There are many definitions of discipline. It is simply the practice of training people to obey certain rules or a code of behavior.

Proverbs 1:2-3 The purpose of Proverbs is to 2. "Teach people wisdom and discipline, to help them understand the insights of the wise. 3. Their purpose is to teach people to live disciplined and successful lives, to help them do what is right, just, and fair". To be disciplined, is to re-train your mind of all the bad habits that we develop through the years. Simply put, what is your daily routine? Self-control is the best form of discipline! Each action we take, comes with a consequence, whether it be positive or negative.

Self-discipline is something that needs to be instilled in our minds and hearts at an early age. There are many benefits to living a disciplined life, it isn't always easy, but eventually, it does pay off and the lasting affect is much more positive then living an un-disciplined and un-healthy lifestyle. If we want to live a rewarding and successful life, we must learn self-discipline. It could be as simple as waking up an hour early to exercise just to get your day going and your blood flowing. Or as simple as spending a few minutes meditating. You'd be surprised at how both boosts your energy levels throughout the day as well as boosts your self-confidence. The benefits of exercising are virtually limitless, not only does it reduce the risk of heart disease, stroke, and high blood pressure, but also will increase your self-esteem and help with stress management. Here are seven benefits of exercise set forth by the Mayo Clinic.

1. Exercise controls weight

Exercise can help prevent excess weight gain or help maintain weight loss. When you engage in physical activity, you burn calories. The more intense the activity, the more calories you burn.

2. Exercise combats health conditions and diseases

Worried about heart disease? Hoping to prevent high blood pressure? No matter what your current weight, being active boosts high-density lipoprotein (HDL), or "good," cholesterol and decreases unhealthy triglycerides. This one-two punch keeps your blood flowing smoothly, which decreases your risk of cardiovascular diseases.

3. Exercise improves mood

Need an emotional lift? Or need to blow off some steam after a stressful day? A gym session or brisk 30-minute walk can help. Physical activity stimulates various brain chemicals that may leave you feeling happier and more relaxed.

4. Exercise boosts energy

Winded by grocery shopping or household chores? Regular physical activity can improve your muscle strength and boost your endurance.

5. Exercise promotes better sleep

Struggling to snooze? Regular physical activity can help you fall asleep faster and deepen your sleep. Just don't exercise too close to bedtime, or you may be too energized to hit the hay.

6. Exercise puts the spark back into your sex life

Do you feel too tired or too out of shape to enjoy physical intimacy? Regular physical activity can improve energy levels and physical appearance, which may boost your sex life.

7. Exercise can be fun ... and social!

Exercise and physical activity can be enjoyable. It gives you a chance to unwind, enjoy the outdoors or simply engage in activities that make you happy. Physical activity can also help you connect with family or friends in a fun social setting.

The reality of implementing a routine of exercise is that only a small percentage will stick to it. Consider all the New Year resolutions you have made in the past, the biggest resolution that people make is related to health. Losing weight and getting in better shape. Truth is, by January 17tth, 90% of those resolutions are already broken for lack of self-discipline. Want to get out of the norm and do something different from what everyone else is doing, then stick to whatever you set your mind to no matter how hard or difficult it is!

It is said that what you put into your mind the first 15 minutes of the day sets the tone for your day. Are you feeding your mind with the negativity of the morning news? Are you rushing around getting ready for work because you don't give yourself enough time to enjoy your morning? Are you in such a hurry that you never have time to eat breakfast to get your energy levels up to where they need to be to get you through the day? These are all self-taught negative habits that we develop through the years that gets us to where we are, sometimes even feeling stuck in that same old rut that we can never seem to dig ourselves out of. It's easy to create habits, but it's harder to break them. Imagine if you would, get up 15 minutes earlier than normal, and you start by positioning your day with positive affirmations. Write down 10 positive affirmations, and read them every morning for one week.

"I am smart"!

"I am a good father/mother"!

"I am a good husband/wife"!

"I am creative"!

"I am wealthy"!

"I am a hard worker"!

"I am a man of God'!

Get the point? You create your affirmations specifically designed for your life. When you tell yourself these things, eventually you are going to start believing it and it will start to affect your life in a positive way. The mind is very powerful, and the more we tell ourselves positive affirmations the more we believe it and then, the more we will implement it into our lives. It takes 21 days to create a habit, and months to break it. Creating positive habits in your life will lead you to being self-disciplined, and in return, will lead you to a happier life.

Now, set a goal for getting up 30 minutes earlier. The first 15 minutes you spend speaking self-affirmations, the next 15 minutes try listening to positive motivational messages on YouTube. There are a variety of speeches and speakers that you can listen to and get many different messages on just about any subject. For me, Les Brown is my go to speaker. Not only does he give you powerful motivational speeches, but they are also backed by biblical practices, which I try to implement into my everyday living. Jim Rohn said it best, "If you want things to change, you have to change"! These are words I live by.

Not a day goes by that I don't start my day with at least two hours devoted for my personal development. Pouring into yourself and developing your mind and body is literally one of the hardest things to change when you have developed so many bad habits throughout the years.

Now that you have devoted the first 30 minutes of your day to yourself, step it up a notch, push for 60 minutes. That's right, an entire hour devoted only to you. Remember, if you want things to change, you must change. You've spent the first 15 minutes of you day reading positive affirmations, the next 15 minutes listening to motivational speeches, and now, try reading a book, your bible, or something that will increase your knowledge. It is said that the average person reads only one book per year, imagine if you read one book per month, that's 12 books per year and 60 books over a period of 5 years, which is equivalent to a college education. Could you just imagine the vast knowledge you would have created within yourself over the last 5 years if you would have put this self-disciplined practice into motion before now? It's never too late to start! You have already positioned yourself with creating two great habits for the 1st 30 minutes of your day, now take it to the next level and discipline yourself with the personal development side of increasing your knowledge with books. Les Brown says, "Knowledge is the new currency", so why stop learning. If you want to be more, you must do more. It is said that you can tell a lot about a person by the size of their library. What's in your library?

The routine that I have created over the past several years has lead me to living a healthier life, being in better physical shape, believing in myself more so now than ever, and creating the desire and thirst for knowledge. It is in the 1st 2 hours of my day that I truly find myself and set myself up for great success. My routine consists of three positive worship songs straight out of bed. It allows me to grow spiritually each, and every day and leads me into my next step, positive affirmations, and then one hour at the gym, to increase my physical health. While at the gym I listen to an hour of motivational speeches, which sets the tone for my day. But I don't stop there. The next step is to read for a minimum of 30 minutes. For me, it's my bible, I have developed a desire to grow not only in every aspect of my life, but also spiritually. Through this, I have gained wisdom, patience, knowledge, and character. This for me is the # 1 personal development book of all time. Now, I do want you to realize, this is just to get my day started, most times by the end of the day I will dig into another book, just for personal gain. One book I strongly suggest reading when you start your transformation is Rick Warren's "The Purpose Driven Life". It is a 40-day reading set forth with 40 chapters that will truly change the way you think and the outlook on your life. It is a great master peace that I firmly believe should be in everyone's library.

As I said before, self-discipline starts with self-control. There are many things that I want to do throughout the day, but I know that in no way would it benefit any aspect of my life. Without self-control I would be grabbing a cookie out of the cabinet every time I walked into the kitchen, but I know that would benefit no-one but Keebler. Think about how many times a week that you stop off at the local convenience store and spend five dollars or maybe more on a soda, candy bar or a bag of chips. Imagine how much money you would save if would just have enough self-control to wait till you got to your destination and drink water and snacked on something healthy. Think about how much bigger your bank account would be if you cut out 80% of your spur-of-the-moment spending, much less should I mention how much healthier you would feel. And your health benefits would be greatly increased. By no means am I saying that we shouldn't treat ourselves every now and again, but every day leads to less retirement savings and a thicker waistline.

If you remember, I mentioned that I was almost at 300 pounds and in the worst shape of my life, at over 40 years young. I didn't have any self-respect for what I put into my body nor did I care about those in my house hold that had the same bad eating habits as I did. It was difficult to change my mindset of my diet and exercise and I always argued the fact that eating healthy was more expensive than that of what I budgeted my household for. Truth be told, it wasn't more expensive to change my eating habits, I just had to create a disciplined mindset that I was going to eat healthier and I was going to take the time to prepare my meals instead of constantly eating takeout or fast food. With that, I set a personal goal to lose 80 pounds. It was tough and by no means did the weight just disappear, I had to have more self-control and track every day what I put into my body and the amount of exercise I did each day. You never really know how bad you feel until you start feeling good. The first 30 days I lost 20 pounds. Wow! And that was with only changing my diet and I started drinking two Herbalife shakes per day, and no exercise had been implemented at that time. And my budget for food did not increase, imagine that, eating healthier, losing weight, and all without spending any more money than what I was already expecting.

Next, I started dedicating one hour at the gym 6 days a week. Sounds like a lot I know, but that was at the time, just one less hour I would spend watching TV. So I cut out the morning news and spent that hour at the gym. Remember, if you want things to change, you must change, and that's exactly what I did, change! Before long it became routine, the weight started to shed, I was feeling better than I had in years, and my appearance started to improve. I slowly started to regain the self-confidence I had in my earlier years and I was determined to not stop. This is something that has become a daily routine for me, and even on the days I just want to stay in bed, I drag myself out, and do it any way. This was just one part of re-training myself to be a better me. Self-control plus self-discipline equals a better quality of life.

What areas of your life do you need more self-control in? It is true that without self-control, it is hard to be self-disciplined. We have become a society of un-disciplined, un-motivated, and entitled people which in return has ruined the essence of discipline. We are easily tempted and fall short on most occasions and take advantage of all the luxuries of the world without thinking about what negative affects it may have on ourselves or others. It is also true that good things come to those that work hard for it, but, in the same respect, too much of a good thing leads us to keeping it all to ourselves and never sharing our gifts or blessings with the world, as it was intended for us to do.

Now, it is time to do self-reflecting and think about areas of your life that you want to change. What bad-habits are you willing to give up in order for you to start living a more disciplined life? Remember, a goal without action is merely a thought, so get serious about this and truly devote yourself to a better, more disciplined life. What factors play a role in your self-control that lead you to fall short of what you know you should or shouldn't be doing. Take back control of your life and rise above where you are currently and strive to be the very best version of you that anyone has ever seen. I know you can do it, because you have greatness within you!

1.What are three disciplined habits that you feel are too difficult and has caused you to feel un-fulfilled.

_____

_____

_____

_____

_____

2. Will these habits benefit your life and those around you? If so, then how?

_____

_____

_____

_____

_____

3.What are three daily routines you can
implement into your life that will help get
you to where you want to be?

_____

_____

_____

_____

_____

4.What is the title to the last book that you read? And did you finish it?

_____

_____

_____

_____

_____

5.What 6 books are you going to set a goal to read in this up-coming year?

_____

_____

_____

_____

_____

Chapter 3 "Ask Yourself, Who Am I, and Who Have I Become"

The 3rd step in Re-inventing yourself is figuring out who you are, and who you have become. Doesn't it seem fair that you have more clarity and a better understanding of who you are? For some, who they have become is not who they wanted to be in life, which has caused them to live life feeling stuck and accepting mediocrity instead of stepping into their greatness. Do you remember, when you were a kid, always being told that you can be anything you want to be when you grow up? That was one of the hardest things for me to process when I was young, because I never really grew up until I was in my 40's. In fact, who I became was what those around me wanted me to be, plus much more, in which I became more of a burden on society than anything. **1 Timothy 4:12 Don't let anyone think less of you because you are young. Be an example to all believers in what you say, in the way you live, in your love, your faith, and your purity.** If only I had read that in my youth, it would have given me the courage that I lacked to becoming whom I was meant to be, instead of what I let society mold me into, or thought there of anyway.

For me, I didn't want to grow up. Growing up scared the crap out of me because I didn't want to be like all those around me. No ambitions, no dreams, no goals, so I took the easy route. I conformed to my environment and became just like all those that was around me. Nobody says they want to be a drug dealer when they grow up! But that's what I became. Nobody says that they want to ruin people's lives when they grow up! But that's what I did. Nobody says they want to neglect their children of their time when they grow up, but that is exactly what I did and who I became. You see, I played the victim, and I did it very well. I became a product of my society and environment and played the part so well that I soon thought of myself as being a victim of circumstance. Taking that road was the easiest for me. It meant that I didn't have to set any goals to get there, and I didn't have to dream to become who in fact, I became.

For such a long period of my life, I really did not care for who I was. I knew deep down that I was not who I was called to be. I lived with no integrity or morals and subjected the world to my pain and darkness. Like I said earlier, I lived a double life. In my teenage years I was a bit of a trouble maker and lived the way I saw fit. I had no care for school or the grades I made, and I graduated only with making a plea to the Board of Education. You see, on senior picture day, I was walking through the parking lot and someone that had already dropped out of school tossed me an open beer, great! I remember to this day, the exact words and voice of my principle, "Mr. Kelley, Mr. Kelley I got you now, come with me". NO! Trouble seemed to find me, because looking back, I always caused trouble. I did not have to take that beer. I could have let it hit the ground and walked away. But that's not who I was at that time in my life. Instead, I chose to accept it. I chose to walk away with it. I made a decision that lead to an even more difficult situation for my life, just like I had done for so many years. It took me five years to get out of high school, and it was by the Grace of God that I did. So, you see, God has had his hand on my life for a very long time. Does any of this sound familiar to you?

There was so many negative events from my past that defined who I was at the time. And it lasted over a period of 2 decades. After I was finally able to be released from high school, I did not stop my path of destruction. I became even more lost in my double identity. I soon got married, had children, and started my search for The American Dream. I had no clue what the American dream was, so I made it up as I went along. Adhering to life the way those around me wanted. My double life led me to be a family man during the day, work hard and provide for my wife and kids. And then, on to my next life at night, continuing to run the streets as I did in my teenage years, dealing destruction and inflicting turmoil on those who I called my friends and family. I had no care for life, not mine nor anyone else's. I saw people's lives being ripped apart and marriage's dissolve and it was all at the hands that dealt addiction! My hands! Considering that this is what I saw growing up, this was the way that I thought life should be. But I always had to take it one step further just to supply my ego and personal self-destruction. Finally, my mind and body had had enough! I hit rock bottom and found myself living in my truck and totally lost. It was time I seek the help that I needed to get my life back from my addiction.

Who I had become was nothing short of being a monster. What I thought of myself was just the same, if not worse. I had created a life built from dishonesty and shame, and found myself in the trenches of hell. For 20 years I lived this life, and it escalated into something uncontrollable, the older I got. I had become a product of my environment and a victim of society all in the same realm. Or at-least this is what I told myself just to get past some of the pain and hurt I felt. Just like everything else I did in my life, I avoided responsibility for my actions and refused to be held accountable. I had no dreams, no goals, no plan of action, not even a thought of being anything other than what I had become. In that very long 20 years, I saw most of my friends either going to prison, or dyeing. But were they truly my friends or just a big part of the problem that I had created. Some of them I still to this day call true friends, and 80% of those have since passed, and some are still in prison. They never had a chance to re-invent themselves, they passed on leaving behind what I, myself, could get out of. It is said that if you show me your 5 closest friends, then that will show exactly who you are. Your circle of influence.

So, let me ask you, who are you? Deep down in the core of your soul, who are you? **Genesis 1:27 So God created human beings in his own image. In the image of God, he created them; male and female.** I was not even close to being who God created me to be. No one knows who you truly are except for you and God. We can all make assumptions, and judgements, but are we truly the ones who are to pass judgement on someone? If you answer that question honestly, is that the person you wanted to become? When people would ask me who I was, my answer would always be Bradley, but that wasn't who I was, that was merely my name. I really didn't want people to know who I really was, I never let my own mother know who I really was. She thought I was a hard-working angel that could do no wrong, but that is a mother's job. To believe in their children, and in her eyes, I was perfect. I was very good at manipulating those around me. Whatever I wanted you to think of me is what you would see. Even though I lived a double life, I was dead on the inside, I was confused, lost, and longed for who I am today. I had no clue who that person was, and it was only with the Grace of God that my identity would be revealed.

"How you define life determines your destiny" Rick Warren

It seems that many people choose the same path that I chose at an early age. Even though each one of us has our own individual story, there are many similarities that cause the same effect on each one of our lives. It creates that feeling of hopelessness, shame, and guilt that we carry around for years, decades, and in some cases, our entire lives. Remember, let go, let God, and find peace? I have found true peace in not becoming who I think I want to be, but in becoming who I know God has called me to be. We are all called to be something of great value in the eyes of our Father, and it is the skills that he allows us to have and develop that will define how we make a living. It is the love he places within us that will allow us to grow into more than what we think we are capable of.

Is it possible to be more without the riches of the world? For so many, wealth of money defines who they are, but are they truly happy and living a fulfilling life? You can have all the money your mind desires, but if your heart is shallow and empty, there will not be one single day that passes that will give you fulfillment of living a truly purposeful life. When you are finally able to let go, then you will start to become whom you were created to be. Are you one whom only thinks of oneself or is everything you do for the greater cause of those around you. We all want great success and wealth, but sometimes, wealth isn't seven or eight figures. Wealth can also be categorized by the influence that you have on not only your life, but of the lives around you and of the world.

"There is no greater feeling in the world than when you can put a smile on somebody's face just by walking in the room. It's unbelievable. And if I have that power, who am I to waste it".

JJ Watts

We all have it within us to light up a room when we walk into it. It shows a true sign that peace has become part of you. We all have it within us to become much more than what we think we are capable of. But are we fully submitting ourselves to become exactly what God has created us to be? We were meant for so much more and often we fall short of our true calling. I often tell myself "I must" and "I will" become what I was created to be. By no means am I where I think I should be, but it is a daily process that gets me further than I was the day before. And it is with God's grace and mercy, I am able to enjoy the journey. You must tell yourself daily that you are becoming whom God has created you to be, and put the past where it belongs which is behind you. Put your very best foot forward and believe first, that God can direct your path, and second, that you believe in yourself enough to step into the greatness that you were called to be. If you can think it, you can do it.

If you were asked, "are you happy with whom you have become"? Could you answer honestly? If you are not, then only you can make the decision to change it. You need to make a direct decision right now to change the path that you are on. Only you and God can change what you have become. Only God knows exactly what you have been through. And it is only by your will that you can submit and let God take control of your life, and lead you down the footsteps that have already been planted by him.

Close your eyes. Vision it. See it. Dream it. Now submit to it, and become it! You need to work hard for whom you want to become. Nothing good comes easy or without sacrifice or dedication. Commit to the person you see yourself as and don't quit becoming that of what you know you can become. You are going to experience failures in life, it is a part of the growth process, and that's ok. Difficulties are also a part of the growth process, nothing great is easy. But how we overcome the adversity of our failures and difficulties will be the defining factor of who we are becoming. You owe it to yourself to get un-stuck and strive to be what you were created to be. You owe it to yourself to become more than what you are and be the person that influences those around you. Step out of your norm, and step into your new.

Exercise:

1.List the 5 most important people in your life.

_____

_____

_____

_____

_____

2.Can you define the person that you have

become in one sentence?

_____

_____

_____

_____

_____

3.Are you truly satisfied with the person

you have become? Why or Why not?

_____

_____

_____

_____

_____

4.What 3 action steps can you take to become the person you want to become?

_____

_____

_____

_____

_____

5.Do you have the discipline to change into the person you want to become?

_____

_____

6.In the blank space below, write down all the things of your past that has led you to who you are today that you are not happy with. Read them aloud and then "Let Go, Let God and find you Peace.

_____

_____

Chapter 4 "Find the Meaning Behind Your Why"

In the 4th step, it is time to analyze our life and decide what it is that we live for. It is true that we all have a "Why". But what truly motivates you and gives you the drive to get up every day and continue to do what it is that you do? We contain within us the power, will, and determination to do anything we set our mind to. But what is the driving force behind what you do? Much of the population's "Why" is to simply live life on their terms and pay their bills. Don't you think that your why should be more meaningful than that? For much of my life I did the same. I had no "Why", other than that of my own selfish needs. I mean, don't get me wrong, yes, I insured, for the most part, that my wife and kids always had a roof over their heads, and the bills got paid. But I never did it for the greater cause of my family. I never even really thought about it. I just did what I did because that was what I believed needed to be done.

In November of 2000, my entire life and world shifted. I submitted my addiction and made the decision to seek the help that I needed and went into a rehabilitation program. For 30 days I learned processes that, at the time, I would need for the rest of my life in order for me to remain sober. I did an entire month of submitting, praying, and soul searching. And truly thought that I was cured. My creative spirit started to reveal itself and I found true peace in words. I was finally able to let go of quite a bit, but not everything. I accepted responsibility for most of my actions that had led me to the place where I was, but 30 days was not near enough to truly forgive and accept 20 years of addiction and destruction. Even though I was able to get sober, for a short time, I still did not realize or even think about my "Why". To give you an idea of where my mind was at the beginning of that 30 days, I will share with you the first piece I wrote three days after arriving:

"Personal Destruction"
There is a problem with corruption
Probably the fact that it will never
change

Waiting and watching for the next
eruption
Looking for somewhere to lay the
blame
Trenching a shallow yet deeper hole
Covering up the worst of pain
Looking up and above personal
destruction
Correcting solutions without any
shame
Noticing sorrow in sizable proportion
Blistering your mind to go insane
To lead and to follow with nowhere to
go
And to go nowhere it's all the same
Holding back from what's known as
right
Knowing it's right will hold you to
refrain
But accepting your wrong will only
be better
No more head-on dancing with a train

The words that would flow out of my

mind was a process of release and led to

more accountability that I would accept.

And the more at peace my heart would be. But even after getting sober, I was still empty with no "Why". I had no clue how many were counting on me. I still had little care about those that were looking up to me. I had no drive to be the best man that I could be. I drug myself out of bed every day, no motivation, just the thought that, man, I got to go to work. I didn't want to go to work. I didn't even like what I did for a living. I just knew it paid the bills. I longed for my passion, but I had no clue what that was. I loved to write, but did nothing after rehab. I loved music, but that lifestyle wasn't good for the family. My "Why" became simply paying the bills and providing for my family. Don't get me wrong, that is a very good "Why", but for me it was unfulfilling. I still felt empty even though I exceled at my job. I knew I was destined for something greater, but what was it that I was in search of?

"Success without fulfillment is failure"!
Tony Robbins

Being a valuable, trustworthy, and hard worker is a great attribute to have, and even the Bible makes many references to working. **Ecclesiastes 9:10 Whatever you do, do well. For when you go to the grave, there will be no work or planning or knowledge or wisdom.** How many times throughout your life have you heard, "you can't take it with you when you die"? This passage truly defines that phrase. We can't in-fact take anything with us when we go. We can re-define our "Why" and leave a legacy that is much more valuable than money. What are you going to be remembered for when you go? There are people around, counting on you. Your "Why" must be greater than just getting up every day and going to work. Your "Why" must leave positive footprints everywhere you go and leave a message of love on all those you encounter.

What is your "Why"? What is the drive behind what gets you out of bed every single day? Is it to be the best father you can be? To be the best leader at your job so you can watch others excel? Is it to deepen your spiritual growth so you can have a more intimate relationship with Christ? There must be more meaning to your life than only living for the selfish needs of yourself. Have you thought about the question, "why do you exist"? What has God put you on this earth for? If you don't know what your "Why" is, then you have no reason to get better and improve yourself at anything you do. Our lives must have substantial meaning when it comes to living out our "Why", and fulfilling God's purpose for us. We were not put on this earth to only live life for ourselves and to only fulfill our own needs. There is more to life than that. Once you find your "Why", then you must do everything in your power to achieve it. If it means working 4 more hours a day on yourself, then do it! If it means that you must get up an hour earlier, then do it! If it is going to require that you give 120% at everything you do, then do it! To many times in life we let our fear of failure rule over our decisions to step out of our ordinary instead of putting our very best foot forward and giving it everything we got! Just do it!

"It's fine to celebrate success, but it is more important to heed the lessons of failure".

Bill Gates

If you think that there will not be failures along the way, then you are wrong. It's how we react to our failures that will turn each one into a success. Failure is a part of life and we are all going to experience it, there is no way around it. But true success and fulfillment of your why will be well worth trying again, and again, and again. I guarantee it.

My why is simple, but it requires a very complex plan of action to achieve it. It is simply to "Change the World One Dream at a Time". Seems impossible, right? They say that by the end of 2017, there will be 7.6 billion people on earth. There is simply no way that I can physically change every single person on earth. It would be humanly impossible. But, there are actions that I can take to ensure that by the time I leave this earthly home and venture into my heavenly home, that I have done everything in my power to accomplish this task. Believing this is even possible has required me to change my way of thinking. Some of those that are around me, I am sure think that I am crazy, and yes, they are correct. I may just be a little crazy believing that someone like me can change the world, but this is my "Why".

By no means would this be possible if I were still stuck in the rut that I was in so long ago. I believe all things are possible with the will and determination that God has put in my heart. **Isaiah 50:7 Because the Sovereign Lord helps me, I will not be disgraced. Therefore, I have set my face like a stone, determined to do his will. And I know that I will not be put to shame.** This is what drives me to get up at 5:00 A.M. every day! This is the factor that makes me work harder on myself than I do on my job! This is what has giving me the determination required for me to write this book. The people of the world need to re-ignite their dreams and a life of passion for everything they do. And we have lost the true essence of passion. Our creative side must be aroused as it once was in our youth. You see, it has simply started with me, and the more that I am able to pour into my family, friends, and everyone I meet, and leave that positive message of hope and that anything is possible, then this simple message will eventually reach the world. It doesn't matter if it happens in my lifetime. It probably never will. But I guarantee I will put my best foot forward and do everything in my power to insure all those around me are enabled with the tools they will need to live a life of greatness and meaning. The world needs to be a better place. People need to know that they can accomplish any dream they can think up, but they must believe in themselves.

Life is going to be full of ups, and downs. You will experience your share of successes and failures. But if you discover our "Why", and you want it as much as you want to breathe, then you can do anything in this world you dedicate yourself to. It doesn't matter how hard you think it may be, it is possible, anything is possible.

"If you always do what is easy, your cup will always be half empty, but if you do what is hard, your cup will always be half full".

Bradley Kelley

Exercise:

1.What is your why?

_____

_____

_____

_____

_____

2.Who is counting on you the most at this

point in your life?

_____

_____

_____

_____

_____

3.What is the drive behind what you do

each day?

_____

_____

_____

_____

_____

4.What roadblocks must you overcome in order to pursue your why?

_____

_____

_____

_____

_____

Chapter 5 "Commit to Your Purpose"

In the 4th step, you were able to identify your "Why" and the reasons behind what makes you do what it is that you do. By now you should have a clear picture of the direction that your life is turning and the impact you want to make in this world. The 5th step is going to require that you really focus on your definition of commitment and stay true to what you set your mind to. I have found that there are many definitions of commitment, but the one that really resonated with me deeply is this; **"Making a commitment involves dedicating yourself to do something, like a person or a cause. Before you make a commitment, think**

carefully. A commitment obligates you to do something".

Vocabulary.com

A commitment obligates you to do something! I cannot even count all the times I ran from obligations. There were so many times that life would get too hard and I would disconnect from my commitment. There is a pain period to everything good in life that we do, but just because it's hard, doesn't mean we run from it. When you commit yourself to your purpose, then you have reached a point in your life where you have an abundant level of determination and passion for what you believe in. Nothing can stop you! It doesn't matter that life will throw you curves at each turning point. You are going to power through the pain. It doesn't matter that you must work harder. You are going to power through the pain. It doesn't matter that the people around you think you are crazy, because they are right, and you are going to power through the pain. And those that stick with you, no matter how crazy you may be, are going to go with you, straight to the top.

So, as I said before, my "Why" has been re-ignited and it is to "change the world one dream at a time", which has created many different purposes. The level of commitment that I put towards each one will define whether my purpose is carried out. My most important purpose here in this life is to insure I have a mature and intimate relationship with Christ. This will allow me to grow in many areas of my life that will place me in positions that I may carry out the many other purposes for my life. **Philippians 4:13 "For I can do everything through Christ, who gives me strength".** If I lean on these words in my weakest moments, it gives me an undeniable amount of strength and hope. It leads me to focus on the bigger picture of my purpose which allows me to dig deep no matter how hard it may be. Because it is fact, this is where my strength comes from. It has taken me a very long time to learn how to put God 1st. Being vulnerable to his calling and living by faith and not just sight is something I often remind myself that I must do daily. Even though most of my life has been built off all the materialistic pleasures of this world, this is a process that requires complete trust in him no matter what my mind may tell me. It's my heart that I must follow. If we learn to put God 1st, it is then he will place before us all the things in life he has already promised us.

The 2nd most important purpose is my family. There is nothing I will not do to ensure that everything I do will be for the greater good of my family. For such a long time I lived with the thought that I let my family down, when, I only let myself down. Their love for me didn't change. They would still do anything for me no matter what it was. Did it hurt them, the life I was living? Absolutely! But it didn't change the fact that they wanted me to succeed in everything I did. When you have dedicated purposes in live, it changes your perspective in how hard you are willing to work to get there. I will not lose! I will not quit! I will be successful! I will change the world! You must believe in your ability to do the things it takes to make your dreams a reality. Life is hard, but it is harder living with the fact that you didn't put your best foot forward at accomplishing everything behind your "Why". My mentor, **Les Brown** says it best. **"You must be willing to do today what others won't do, in order to have the things tomorrow others won't have".** Tell yourself this every day! And when you get sick of hearing it, do it again, and again, until it becomes your reality. You must take mediocrity completely out of your vocabulary to step into your greatness.

If everything we do is to only fulfill our own needs, then what good would it do to make a positive impact on others. My 3rd greatest purpose is to ensure that every single person I meet knows their true value and potential. Some of you do not realize exactly how great you are. You fail to realize that without you, your friends and family would be left with an emptiness in their hearts. It is up to you whether you live out your true purpose, and it's up to you the impact you have on people's lives. Isn't it time that you started living life to be the best that you can be in all that you do? You must live life full. You must remove any doubt in your mind that you will not succeed. You must, because it is possible.

What is it that you want out of life? What is it that scares you about committing to what you want? Fear is the number one killer of our hopes and dreams. Fear is the deciding factor between success and failure. Fear is in fact, the only thing that stands between you and living out your greatness. Take fear out of the equation, now what is your excuse. I love it when I hear someone say they are going to try. My children would tell me they were going to try, but there was fear and doubt behind what they were saying. If you are completely confident in your ability, then there is no try. They very quickly learned that my immediate response to them would be; "trying is a mouthful of failure, either you do it or you don't". I am going to try to be successful! No, you are going to be successful. I am going to try to leave a legacy for my children! No, you are going to leave a legacy behind for your children. I am going to try to pay my rent! No, you are going to get kicked out if you don't pay your rent. Let me tell you from experience, the easiest way to get back on your feet is to get your car repoed! That will get you back on your feet quicker than anything in this world. Maybe you should have tried a little harder to make your car payment.

How do you commit your time? What do you do with the 24 hours in each day that we all have? It is true that we all have the same 24 hours in a day, but it is what we do with those 24 hours that define our success. For many years I worked 12 hours a day, 5 days a week, and sometimes even 6 days a week. I made a good living for the most part. I made sure my bills were paid. But I invested 12 hours into someone else's dream, and none for my own. Made them millions of dollars, and in return for all the hard work and dedication I was able to make a much smaller amount for my own. I am not telling you to quit your job, nor am I telling you not to work hard, but don't let your career and job prevent you from accomplishing your dreams. I didn't commit to my dreams, I committed to theirs. I had 16 hours left in that day, you know that I had to sleep for at least 6 to 8 hours of that time, so what did I do with the other 4 to 6 hours of that day? You would think I committed it to my kids and family, but I did not. You would like to think that I spent at least an hour devoted for my own development, but again, I did not. I was not committed to my family with my time, nor was I committed to setting goals and chasing my dreams. I had no dreams!

So, what is your purpose? How many reasons can you think of that make you want to change what you are doing and work harder at being the best version of you? Quit doubting yourself because it is going to be hard. Life is hard. But don't you think that you would at least like to say that you did the very best you could and failed, instead of not even trying and fail? It's time you peel back those layers and figure out what is truly holding you back from committing to your purpose and bringing to life your why. It's time you quit making excuses of why you can't step out of your comfort zone and shoot for the moon. To this day, my kids remember me telling them that, "you need to shoot for the moon in everything you do, because if you miss, at least you will land amongst the stars". I gave great advice back then, if only I had listened to my own words.

Exercise:

1.What are you top 3 purposes in life?

_____

_____

_____

_____

_____

2.Describe your level of commitment in the past.

_____

_____

_____

_____

_____

3.What are 3 challenges you must overcome to commit to your purpose?

_____

_____

_____

_____

_____

4.What kind of legacy are you committed to create for those around you?

Chapter 6 "Dream Big and Set Even Bigger Goals"

In the 6ᵗʰ step of this process we are going to learn how to dream as we once did in our youth, and set goals to achieve those dreams. The only difference is that right now, at this point in your life, I am sure you have already experienced some failures that will not prevent you from being able to "dare to dream". It is possible for you to dream beyond your wildest imagination and set goals associated with giving life to those dreams. "Dare to dream". You see, we all have experienced our share of failures that has caused us to give up on our dreams. Some of the pain we have been through has thrown up a wall, preventing us from ever daring to dream again. Do you realize that just as fear distracts you from your purpose, doubt will crush your dreams before they are even acknowledged? When your mind is filled with doubt and fear, you will never have the courage to get out of your comfort zone. You will never be able put faith in yourself to have the ability to be successful.

Habakkuk 2:2 The Lord answered me: Write down this vision; clearly inscribe it on tablets so it may be easily read. Before a dream can become reality we first must vision it. You must be able to clearly see what it is that you want, no matter how big or small it is. Without a clear vision, your desire to achieve it will never be strong enough to push you through the pain period of making your dreams a reality. If you don't see it, before you see it, you are probably never going to see it! Once you got a vision of your dreams, write it down. Look at it every single day. You see, words are very powerful. I cannot talk enough about the power of words. Just as self-affirmations are important, so are claiming your dreams and goals as if you have already accomplished them. This is very important If you want something bad enough. You are going to speak it into existence. How bad do you want it? You must wake up every single day and tell yourself, I will fulfill my dreams today. You must wake up every single day and tell yourself, "today is my day". "Today is your day"! You've quit living in the past. "Today is your day". You finally forgave yourself.

"Today is your day". We are all going to stumble at times, maybe even fall flat on our face, but we must get up. People our counting on you to fulfill your dreams. The world is counting on you to succeed. You must ask yourself; "What do I want to become and what price am I willing to pay to get there"?

"Keep your eyes on the stars and your feet on the ground".

Teddy Roosevelt

I have always been a dreamer. Ever since I can remember I was always dreaming about something. The problem always lied in the fact that I never had anyone tell me that I can do it. Or maybe I was just too scared to ever tell anyone of my dreams

107

and goals. Again, fear. I never really thought that God would complete what he had already started in me. We all need someone to believe in us. We all need someone to look up to. Again, we need God as our pilot.

"If you can dream it, you can do it".

Walt Disney

Everything in this world has started with a dream. Then turns into a goal. Then turns into a process of steps. Then eventually, becomes a reality. If you can think it, you can achieve it. We are all born with a vivid imagination and a creative genius. But life has a way of throwing us curve balls that lead our thoughts to go out of bounds and stay there. But it is in these steps that we can learn to avoid the realities of life getting us stuck and place in our arsenal the tools we need to continue to press towards our dreams.

There is no amount of words that anyone can say to you that should prevent you from continually pursuing your dreams. If I were to tell you that you will be broke the rest of your life. Are you going to believe me? If I were to tell you that you will never own your own home. Are you going to believe me? What if I told you that you will never be better than what you already are. Will you believe me then? NO! You must remove all the negative from your life and fill it up with scripture, knowledge, and surround yourself with people who want you to succeed.

"You must modify your dreams or magnify your skills"

Jim Rohn

I will not conform to the realities of other people and neither should you! I will be a success in all that I do, and so should you! I will not stop until I change the world one dream at a time, as well, neither should you. Every day you must invest in yourself! Sharpen your mind and your skillset. If all you ever hear from those around you is negative self-talk, then you need to find a new set of friends. It is what we hear from those around us that prevent us from moving forward in our lives. Dare to dream big.

Now that we have a clear vision of our dreams, what's next? For your dreams to become a reality, you must set clear and concise goals. This is the step that will set you apart from creating the life that you know you deserve or just leaving you stuck where you are right now. This is not going to be easy. This is going to require that you work hard to get there. There will come moments when you want to quit, but you have the determination to accomplish anything. There is nothing in this world that can stop you from achieving your goals and dreams. A goal is simply the object of your ambition. If you want to meet the desired result you vision, you must stop at nothing to accomplish this. Setting goals should be a part of life. Anything good comes from having a clear vision and setting steps to complete over a specific period to get to your desired result. You must become outcome oriented. If you look around you, everything you see exist because someone had a vision, that turned into a dream, that became a reality by setting goals. There is nothing that sets you apart from anyone great in this world.

"Whether you think you can or you can't, your right".

Henry Ford

Let's break this down in a few easy steps that you can start doing right now. First set an "Outcome Goal". This is typically a long-term goal that you probably will not be able to accomplish overnight. Say for instance, you want to buy a house. Set a time frame. Within the next two years, you want to be a homeowner. You know it takes money for the down payment and a good credit score. So how much money do you have right now? What is your credit score? Each one you need to increase. Your savings and your credit score. Now let's set "Performance Goals". These are what you need to focus on to achieve your "Outcome Goal", a down payment and a good credit score. Then you must take daily steps to achieve your "Performance Goals", these are called "Process Goals". For instance, instead of eating out five nights per week, you limit yourself to one night per week and put the money you save in a savings account for your down payment. It's the sacrifices we make that will allow us to accomplish anything good in this life. You must become a penny pincher. No more stopping at the store for an energy drink and a bag of chips, for you have already made a conscious decision to be more disciplined in chapter 2. Now put it into practice.

Now that you have already started to save up for your down payment, it's time to work on your credit score. The 2nd of your "Performance Goals". By no means am I telling you how to build your credit, but there are processes you can take to improve your credit score. For me personally, it's to stop maxing out the credit cards and keep the balances low. But this is something that you might seek a credit counselor for. It is a daily process to protect your credit, which would be a "Process Goal". These are daily steps you take for the demand of each "Performance Goal". Make sure all your bills are paid. Insure you do not take out any unnecessary loans, and if you do, pay them on time, but again, I am no credit counselor. Do you get the point? **Joshua 1:8 Study this book of instruction continually. Meditate on it day and night so you will be sure to obey everything written in it. Only then will you prosper and succeed in all you do.**

For each one of your goals, write them down. Place them where you can see them every day. It brings about a feeling of ownership. You own your dreams and your goals. When you fulfill one of your goals, mark it off. It brings about a sense of accomplishment and achievement. Which in return will bring you more self-confidence. You see, these are processes in life that we miss. These are the victories that we fail to celebrate. You must celebrate your victories in life and reward yourself for the achievements. Rewarding ourselves will make the daily struggle more valuable and give us more determination to get over the hurdles in life. Dare to dream. And dare to think bigger than you have ever done before. Because you can do all things through Christ, who gives you strength.

Exercise:

1.List the dreams that died within you because of the fear associated to accomplish them.

_____

_____

_____

_____

_____

2.List three goals you must accomplish to
bring your dreams to reality.

_____

_____

_____

_____

_____

3.Do you have a clear vision of these

dreams?

_____

4.What are the processes you must take to

attain each goal?

117

_____

_____

_____

_____

_____

5.Give specific time frames for each of the three goals.

_____

_____

_____

_____

_____

It's Possible!

Chapter 7 "Stay True to Yourself and Enjoy the New You"

Hebrews 12:13 So take a new grip with your tired hands and stand firm on your shaky legs. Mark out a straight path for your feet. Then those who follow you, though they are weak and lame, will not stumble and fall but will become strong. There is not one person on earth who can change their past or where they come from. Our past is what it is and has directed us to become the person we have become. Every footstep of our life has already been placed before us to follow no matter how hard it was, and no matter the train wreck we went through. Our past doesn't matter. It made us who we are. What matters is what are we going to do with our now, our today, and our future? Just as the stars are aligned in the sky, your life has a place in this world to make a positive difference and impact on people's lives.

Never once in my life was I ever ashamed of who I was or where I came from. I did however, know that I had not discovered my true purpose in this life and that there was in fact, something missing. There was a reason that God kept me out of prison and prevented me from being buried six feet under. For years I thought I was staying true to who I was, but that wasn't really me. That wasn't who I wanted to become. That was simply my perception of the reality that I lived. Fact is, we all have a choice in becoming who we want to be. But we must live that life with the utmost dignity and respect in order that our lives take on true meaning and truly feeds our soul. Live a life that you can be proud of. Live a life that allows you to be yourself for whom you were created to be. It is possible to become more. It is possible to be more. It is possible!

Be true to yourself, help others, make each day your masterpiece, make friendships a fine art, drink deeply from good books – especially the Bible, build shelter against a rainy day, give thanks for your blessings, and pray for guidance every day.

John Wooden

It's time you start being yourself, everyone else is taken. It's time you quit living life like it's a popularity contest, not everyone is going to like you. Quit being a people pleaser! We are all created differently. Each one of us has our own set of skills and purposes for this life, build off each one of them.

You can't be great at each and everything you want to do, but you can be good at everything and great at one or two. It doesn't take a genius to make an impact on this world, or to leave a legacy. But it does take hard work and persistence. Anything good in life does not come easy. But if you work hard and smart, you can reach your greatness, all the while being true to yourself, and being the person, you know you are meant to be.

I have seen all too often people who are worried about being themselves because of what someone else may think. Quit living for their approval. You are not living for them. They don't write your future. Their opinion is not your reality. You were created to be who you are. You may not be proud of some of the things you have done, but be proud of who you are and what you are becoming. You may not be the smartest person in the room, I never was, but I walk with my head held high, back straight, and with dignity. As well as should you. You can always tell a confident person by the stride in their step, be that person that breathes confidence. Be true to who you are. You can become the person you want to be no matter any obstacle placed before you, you were created for greatness, now claim it!

Claim your success in everything you do. Take responsibility for your success and your failures. Take responsibility for your actions and decisions no matter the cost. Don't take life lightly, and be serious about your destination. You can become more than you have ever imagined, but you must remain true to yourself. You can live by the principles you set forth for yourself, but you must remain true to the discipline required to live them. You can pave the way for all those looking up to you, but you must plant positive seeds of growth for those around you to flourish. Life is meant to live in abundance, and I am not talking about an abundance of money or materialistic positions. **Proverbs 36:8-9 You feed them from the abundance of your own house, letting them drink from your river of delights. For you are the fountain of life, the light by which we see.**

It is said that money doesn't make the world go around, and it is true. Love is what makes the world go around. Love and be loved. I take great pride in the fact that I can love the way I do. This is my true self, this is being true to who I am. I am proud of the fact that even though some may talk about me behind my back, my love for them is no less than it was before they gossiped about me. This is my true identity. I will celebrate my failures as well as my successes, for they are the building blocks to my greatness. This is me being true to myself. Be yourself, no one is going to do it for you.

Embrace every thought, and every idea you think of. It doesn't matter how eccentric it may be, it is yours. Run with it. Be true to yourself. Love God as much as you do yourself, it will allow you to love others deeply. Stay true to yourself. Don't run before the miracle happens, in time, it will happen. This requires you to be true to yourself. And reward yourself for your accomplishments, no matter how big or small the victory. Again, you must always stay true to yourself. Be persistent in all that you do. Remember, what the mind can dream, the heart can achieve.

"Six Key Principles to Succeed"

1.Put the "Intense" back into "Intensity"!

2.Develope your mind, and then your skills!

3.Work harder on yourself then you do your job!

4.Be persistent, remember persistence breaks resistance!

5.Think, outside the box, never let the box block you in!

6.The world is here for your taking, take what you need, and give away even more.

Made in the USA
Columbia, SC
28 March 2021

35167647R00072